Tapestry Of Feelings

Irene Wilson

BookLeaf
Publishing

India | USA | UK

Made with ❤ on the BookLeaf Publishing Platform

www.bookleafpub.in

www.bookleafpub.com

Dedication

To the love, the loss, the laughter, and the longing—
You have all been my muses.
and to you,May these words find you where you are
meant to be.

Preface

I have always believed that emotions have voices —some loud, some quiet, some on the edge of silence. They arrive unannounced, settle in our chests, and weave themselves into the fabric of who we are. This collection is their story.

These pages hold love in its purest form—soft and wild, fleeting and endless. They echo with laughter, the kind that bubbles up like spring water, refreshing and light. They carry the weight of sadness, the kind that lingers in the spaces between words. Confusion dances here, too, twisting and turning, lost but never still. And then, there is the feeling of being overwhelmed, where joy and sorrow collide in a storm we struggle to name.

Each poem is a conversation, an outstretched hand, a mirror reflecting the moments that shape us. My hope is that, somewhere in these lines, you find your own emotions speaking back to you.

— Irene wilson

Acknowledgements

This book is a tapestry woven from emotions, and it would not have been possible without the love, support, and inspiration of so many.

To the people who have walked beside me through love, laughter, sadness, and uncertainty

,

thank you for giving me the moments that shaped these words.
Your presence, whether fleeting or constant, has left an imprint on these pages.

And to you, the reader—thank you for opening this book, for allowing these words to be a part of your journey. If even one line resonates with your heart, then this collection has found its true purpose.

1. Summertime love

Summertime love
Filled with giggles and hugs
Silly smiles late night cuddles
Making time go slow
Replaying all along,
A blissful mood around
Wishing for it to never
come to an end ,
Holding on tight with
fleeting whispers and touches
Summertime love
Never letting go
always a precious moment
Closed away in a song.

2. Moon

Soo pretty
Yet Soo far away
Out of my reach,
making it seem like a breaths away
You leave me in awe
Every time I look at you,
Your beauty unmatched
Always bright and glowing
My moon ,
I love you always .

3. Home

My sweet angel
Always by me
through the storms
Your sweet honey eyes
Crinkle when you smile
Always welcoming me
To my home .

4. Blossom

Warmth enveloped the other
As soon as they set their sight on each other,
It felt as if spring bloomed early,
Making the coldness fade away.

Lost in each other put them in an unending trance ,
Making them crave for the other
With a feeling that they'll Never get enough of .

Making them want to be stuck in that spring trance ,
Enveloped with warmth.
Wanting time to freeze with cherry blossoms falling all
around,
Walking hand in hand
Under the flushed sky.....

5. -?-

Heart is a tricky thing
It breaks, it heals
sometimes even stuck
Heart is a tricky thing
That it has a mind of its own
It leaves wanting more,
Heart is a tricky thing
It's confusing yet full of awe .

6. Shooting Star

A Sky full of stars
Yet I wish upon the shooting star
Help me out here
Pull me up ,
Nothing but the sound of night
Just me and the twinkling sky,
Laying down by the cliff
Bustling of the winds
Mind void of thoughts ,
Just wishing upon the shooting star
Help me out here
Pull me up .

7. Rush

Everything goes by in a rush
Not a moment to stop and breathe
Blurring trees ,crowded seas
The push and pull of tiredness
Clinging like a leech,
Anxiety crippling and gripping
The fear of slipping,
Just going on Not knowing
where this path is headed.

8. Waves

Breeze soo light and free
Carries whispers of the sea
Singing songs of their own
waves embrace the shore
Like a timeless dance,
A warm embrace
Away from the hustle and bustle
A quite place ,
Where worries drift away
Along with the tide...

9. Yellow

In world full of greys
You're my yellow
My best friend
My yellow,
The rush of joy when our eyes meet
Makes my heart all warm and fuzzy
Cause, in world full of greys
You're my yellow .

10. Wildflower

Love soo wild, like moon shone bright,
Dancing free in golden light.
No bounds, just endless sky,
Hearts always intertwined.

11. Heart

the heart steady and strong
dancing to its never ending song
in love, so wild, so free
burning away endlessly.

I stretch, I bend, I break, I mend,
A storm, a sun, a foe, a friend.
even when the world feels wrong,
I hope and I move along.

12. A stop

Random thoughts fill our minds
Bouncing around like a ball
many what if's
many should i's
A never ending train of thoughts
Without a station to stop,
it's happy, it's sad
sometimes you don't know
Just going with the flow
Hoping it would finally find
a destination to stop.

13. Chaos

Hustling and bustling
Chaos ensues In my mind
Just like how it is
In the the big cities,
A start point waiting
But what the end is
Will always be a mystery,
Do we choose that path
Do we take their hand
What Do we do?
Creased brows,Puzzled stance
Will we ever know
What truly lies
Beyond the start point,
We trust our gut
Move forward
as the seasons pass by
Looking for answers
To our many questions....
Will we ever know?.....

14. What if

What if it's the last of it
And everything is crumbling down
Nowhere to go no one to hold onto
Spaces closing in on you and
Trapping you in an in ending spiral .

What if we are lost in our own battles
And never find peace with ourselves .
Making us think it's the end ,
the road has come to an end .

What if we are never found
Would we be stuck in the unending maze,
Trying to fight our way through the daze.
What if we aren't pieced back together,
And remain broken as a shattered glass.
Will we ever be pulled out from the darkness into the
light ,
Finding our solace after winning the fight .
What if .....

15. Growing through the cracks

Never meant to bloom here,
Between stone and silence,
Where the earth is dry,
Where there is no whisper of wind.

But I rise
Stubborn as a stem
Roots all tangled uo,
Petals kissed by defiance.

Here I stand,
A wildflower in the ruins,
Growing through the cracks.

16. Midnight hush

Words spill like stardust between us,
soft and unhurried,
as if the night is listening in on us.

Laughters all hushed and mellow
shadows of secrets enveloping
We speak of dreams too big ,
fears too fragile

The night stretching endlessly
The clock forgotten
Just hushed up voices
Bouncing off the walls

And when silence finally settles,
it is not empty but full
with everything we said,
and everything we didn't.

17. Stay

Listen carefully and see
the leaves quiver in the wind,
the sky become a blush as darkness descends,
and the sound of laughter echoing for an extra second.

The only sound
you'll hear is the slow, steady hum of life as it happens,
one beat at a time.

So stay.
Let the world spin,
let time pass like a gentle tide.
For now, just be.

18. Faded Ink

Some people enter like poetry,
soft lines written in the margins of your life,
whispers of something beautiful,
something meant to last—
but not everything reaches its final page.

You hold their words like faded ink,
rereading what was,
imagining what could have been.
But maybe some stories are meant to stay open,
unfinished, unwritten

This collection is a journey through love, loss, joy, and the in between the moments that shape us, the feelings we struggle to name. From the warmth of love's quiet gestures to the weight of words left unsaid, these poems are an invitation to feel deeply, to embrace every emotion, and to find beauty in both the light and the dark.

ABOUT THE AUTHOR

Inspired by everyday experiences, fleeting memories, and the complexity of the human heart, I write to remind readers that they are not alone in their emotions. Whether exploring the softness of love, the weight of sadness, or the beauty of simply existing, their words aim to be both a refuge and a reflection..

9789369540846

Only
SILLY
Things!

A Collection of Hilarious Poems

Arshia Singh